TRAVAIL:

POWERFUL, SUPERNATURAL PRAYER

TRAVAIL: Powerful, Supernatural Prayer

ISBN: 978-1-60920-025-1

Printed in the United States of America

©2011 by Emilie A. Parsons

Cover design by Ajoyin Publishing, Inc.

Library of Congress Cataloging-in-Publication Data

Ajoyin Publishing, Inc.

P.O. 342

Three Rivers, MI 49093

www.ajoyinpublishing.com

Please direct your inquiries to admin@ajoyinpublishing.com

TRAVAIL:

POWERFUL, SUPERNATURAL PRAYER

by

Emilie A. Parsons

Ajoyin Publishing, Inc.
PO Box 342
Three Rivers, MI 49093
1.888.273.4JOY
www.ajoyinpublishing.com

"My little children, of whom I travail in birth again until Christ be formed in you..."

(GALATIANS 4:19)

CONTENTS

CHAPTER 1   PROPHECY GIVEN BY PASTOR   1

CHAPTER 2   A DISASTER BECOMES MY SALVATION   5

CHAPTER 3   TRAVAIL—A POWERFUL GIFT   9

CHAPTER 4   A NEW GIFT—THE HOLY LAUGHTER   15

CHAPTER 5   TWO MORE GIFTS: THE HOLY SILENCE AND SONGS OF WORSHIP   19

CHAPTER 6   SPIRITUAL BIRTHING   21

CHAPTER 7   THE GIFT OF VISIONS   25

CHAPTER 8   LISA'S ACCIDENT   29

CHAPTER 9   WATERWAYS   33

CHAPTER 10   THE VISION OF THE LORD'S ROBES   39

CHAPTER 11   WATER INTO WINE   41

CHAPTER 12   WATERWAYS MEETING   45

CHAPTER 13   PRAYER MEETING AT SISTER JEANNE'S   49

CHAPTER 14   SKY ANGEL   53

CHAPTER 15 A DIVINE APPOINTMENT   57

CHAPTER 16 SPENDING TIME IN INTERCESSION TOGETHER 61

CHAPTER 17 SHARON, A FRIEND OF SHARON'S, AND
            MYSELF BEFORE THE LORD   65

CHAPTER 18 SHARON AND I BEFORE THE LORD   67

CHAPTER 19 SURPRISE   71

CHAPTER 20 NOTES FROM MY JOURNAL   73

CHAPTER 21 THE HOLY HUSH   77

CHAPTER 22 EYES TO SEE   83

CHAPTER 1

PROPHECY GIVEN BY PASTOR FRANGIPANE

"I would say unto you, My people, yea, I have sent weeping and I send weeping-travail-upon My people, for this nation and for the nations. Yea, I have sent laughter and now I say unto you, I am sending weeping and I am sending mourning upon My people, to declare unto Me that, yea, this nation has sinned and, yea, there is sin in the church.

"And so, therefore, I am bringing a brokenness to the heart of the church, a loosening of those things which have bound the hearts of My people, that My people's hearts might be softened; that their ears may be filled with the word of the Lord to hear the burden of the Lord; that their eyes may be filled with

the tears and the crying and the burden of the Lord
for the sins of My people; that a spirit of repentance
would come; that a spirit of crying and weeping and
mourning would come.

"Yea, that I might heal My people, and, yea, so that
I might set My people free and bring deliverance to
this nation and bring deliverance to My church and
set the captives free," saith the Lord. "For My heart
is for you to be on your knees. With weeping and
crying, truly I shall bring forth a revival in this
nation. Yea, and a reformation to this nation, but it
will not come without travail; it will not come without
weeping and without crying and mourning for the
sins of this nation.

"Now come up before Me and, I would say unto you,
when you do this I shall see and take your tears and
I shall bottle them up and pour them out upon you.
There shall be a great fire come forth as never before
that shall bring healing.

"For I say unto you, when My Son wept did He not
next raise Lazarus from the grave? Then I would say
unto you, yea, there shall be a healing; there shall
be a raising of the dead of this nation; there shall be
miracles go forth; there shall be all the restoration
of My church.

"But I am saying unto you, there shall be intimacy
before there will be that. And there will only be intimacy when you come unto Me with travail; when
you come unto Me with brokenness; when you come
unto Me and see and know My heart. For I shall bring
you into that place of intimacy that you've longed for.
For in that place of intimacy, I say unto you, I shall

then bring forth authority to you and you shall do signs and wonders. You shall know the joy of the Lord, but you shall know how I have wept for this nation!"

CHAPTER 2

A DISASTER BECOMES MY SALVATION

Ireceived salvation at the age of 41 during a time of great devastation and upheaval in my life. I was going through a divorce that I did not want. One day I was in my basement in a little office study room. In my utter despair, I fell to the carpeted floor. I could actually see dark clouds all around me as I lay there on the floor. From the depths of my soul, I cried out to God for help.

The next morning I heard a scripture playing in my mind like a recording over and over. It was as if a microchip had been implanted in my brain. "But seek ye first the kingdom of God, and his righteousness; and all these things shall be added unto you" (MATTHEW 6:33). I heard this scripture over and over all my waking hours. Finally I blurted out a request to God, "Tell me how; I don't know how to seek Your kingdom!"

I had been involved in the New Age movement for twenty years. I studied the primary scriptures of Hinduism, all six systems, as well as those of Buddhism. I took courses at the University of Wisconsin on Asian philosophy and was a member of a New Age group. At the time this was happening, I was deep into Zen Buddhism. In my hour of need, none of these philosophies offered any power to help me.

Not long before hearing this scripture, I was talking on the phone to a very dear aunt about my difficulties. She asked if I would like to receive Jesus. I replied that I would take any help I could get. Little did I know that I became born again. I was still very steeped in the Eastern philosophies.

Within a day or two of asking God to show me how to seek His kingdom, my next-door neighbor came over and invited me to a charismatic prayer meeting at his church ,and I went to it. I knew nothing about it, but I was willing to learn. First there was praise and worship. I didn't know why people were raising their hands during worship, but I thought "when in Rome, etc." So I did too.

Then the speaker began to give words of knowledge. (I didn't have a clue what this was at that time.) When he said something to the effect that someone here needs to let go of the past, I knew in my heart that the word was for me. I thought to myself, "How in the world does he know that?" After the meeting my neighbor encouraged me to have prayer with the speaker, so I did. I told him of my situation regarding the divorce. He had his wife put her hand on my heart, then my hand on hers, then he put his hand on mine and prayed for healing of a broken heart. At that meeting I met a precious, spirit-filled woman who prophesied over me. I could not believe that the Lord would speak to me, as I felt like such a failure. I was totally amazed. Nor did I have any idea what a personal God He is, but I was launched into a truly new life. This wonderful, anointed woman mentioned that she was going to another prayer group in a few days, and I asked if I could go with her. I did and there found a spirit-filled prayer group that became my family in the Lord. They nurtured and taught me for five years. It was there that I met the man who was to become my new husband.

The Lord opened many doors for me in the entire charismatic movement in Milwaukee. Besides going to church on Sunday, I went to four prayer meetings during the week. I called it going to the University of the Holy Spirit. I, of course, learned that I needed to have my mind renewed to the Word of God. It was a terrific shock to discover that everything I learned in New Age teachings was not of the one true, living God. The god I learned about was not the very personal God of Abraham, Isaac, and Jacob. I also learned that we have an adversary, Satan, who is a liar and deceiver, and as Jesus said, he came to steal, kill, and destroy (JOHN 10:10A). He also comes as an angel of light and can make evil look good.

I took a Life in the Spirit seminar and received the baptism of the Holy Spirit. After that, as I read scripture, it seemed like the words of truth would light up like neon lights. Jesus told me He would reveal Himself in His word and He did. He is the Word become flesh.

Going through a divorce and coming out of the New Age movement was a double whammy. At times I felt like I was being pulled through knotholes.

Did I do everything right? No, I did not. I stumbled and fell and learned to run to God right away, confess (1 JOHN 1:9), and repent. I learned how to receive forgiveness.

It was such a time of upheaval. I needed to be in prayer and scripture daily. The Lord told me that the enemy does not let go easily. As the song *Amazing Grace* says, "Through many dangers toils and snares I have already come."

I learned about tithing, but my only income was support money for my children and help from my parents. I could not give much, but I promised the Lord the firstfruits of my day. From the time I was born again, I spent at least two hours in the morning in prayer and scripture. I was so hungry for the word and my need to talk to God was so great that I had no trouble praying for two or three hours a day.

CHAPTER 3

TRAVAIL—
A POWERFUL GIFT

The first time I received travail, my husband and I were praying for my son when all of a sudden I felt the power of God move upon me, bringing forth weeping and tears. My husband, not knowing it was a work of the Spirit, rebuked a spirit of grief. I motioned him to stop praying against it, knowing that if I spoke the Holy Spirit would lift. It continued for a while, and then it lifted and the weeping ceased. It was an amazing experience to feel that power and know that the weeping did not originate within me. At the time I did not know it was a form of intercessory prayer called travail. I remembered a woman in a prayer meeting years earlier who witnessed that the Lord had given her a burden to pray for someone, and she lay on the floor weeping for the person. I thought what I had received was something similar to what she described.

Little did I know the amazing journey that God had begun, nor did I understand the magnitude, significance, and power of the gift He had placed within me. After that first time, I began to receive travail whenever I put on praise music and worshipped the Lord. When this mighty presence came upon me, I would lay prostrate on the floor on my face as the weeping came forth. During this time the Lord gave me two scriptures to confirm what He was doing. They were both from the book of Micah, which I had not as yet read, so I was very excited to receive the confirming word of the Lord.

The first scripture is Micah 4:10, "Be in pain, and labour to bring forth, O daughter of Zion, like a woman in travail." The second scripture is Micah 5:3a, "Therefore will he give them up, until the time that she which travaileth hath brought forth;".

Many people in the church are not familiar with and do not understand travail. I certainly didn't until I began to receive it and came to realize how powerful it is.

Travail is an aspect of intercession, which is given by God and is not something we can make happen.

Webster's Dictionary defines to intercede as "to go or pass between, to act between parties with a view to reconcile those who differ or contend: to interpose; to mediate or make intercession; mediation."

The biblical definition is to seek the presence and hearing of God on behalf of others.

The *New Expanded Webster's Dictionary* defines travail as "To labor; to toil, to suffer the pangs of childbirth. –n. labor; severe toil; childbirth." The Greek word for travail is *odino* which means to experience the pangs of childbirth.

Travail is an aspect of prayer that births things in the spirit. JOHN 7:38 says, "He that believeth on me, as the scripture hath said, out of his belly shall flow rivers of living water. The Greek word for belly is *koilia* which means womb.

The principal Hebrew words for travail or giving birth are *yalad* (yaw-lad) and *chuwl* (khool). The word for giving birth in MICAH 4:10 and 5:3 is *yalad* which means to bear young, bear, beget, birth, to bring forth. *Chuwl* means to writhe in pain, especially of parturition (childbirth), to bring forth. In ISAIAH 66:8, "As soon as Zion travailed she also brought forth her sons," the word for travail is chuwl. In ISAIAH 66:8B, "for as soon as Zion travailed, she brought forth her children," the word for travail is *chuwl*.

Travail is brought about by the Holy Spirit. ROMANS 8:26 applies to this form of intercession: "Likewise the Spirit also helpeth our infirmities: for we know not what we should pray for as we ought: but the Spirit itself maketh intercession for us with groanings which cannot be uttered." The prayers brought forth by the Holy Spirit transcend our own knowledge and ability. They are perfect prayers from the heart of the Father.

Once when I was receiving travail for another intercessor who was preparing to leave for China to teach, the tears were falling on her arm. She related to me very excitedly that the Lord revealed to her that the tears were the anointing. They were God's tears, not my own. The key to such intercession is to yield to and cooperate with the Holy Spirit.

For quite some time I was receiving travail at home during my daily worship. Many times the weeping was prolific, and as I lay on the floor on my face before God the carpet became wet from the tears.

In addition to church and prayer meetings, I also attended Aglow meetings. Not long after I received the Lord, a woman in my church invited me to a Women's Aglow Fellowship meeting as it was called then. Now it is known as Aglow International and is an interdenominational organization of Christian women, although men are welcome as well and there are men's Aglow fellowships. Aglow is one of the largest women's associations in the world, with more than four thousand local fellowships meeting together each month in 171 nations. Part of Aglow's mission is to lead women to Jesus Christ and provide them with opportunities to grow in their faith and minister to others. The meetings usually consist of praise and worship, a message from a speaker and a special time of ministry to pray for the needs of the women.

After moving to Florida, I was so happy when I met a wonderful sister in the Lord who hooked me up with Aglow again.

I was used to having the travail at home, so I was quite surprised when I received it at an Aglow International meeting during praise and worship. I whispered, "Oh, Lord, I can't do that here. There are other people around." So I did not release the travail, and immediately a young woman in a wheelchair was brought into the room. The Spirit impressed upon me that the intercession was for her. I felt so terrible and convicted for not obeying and releasing the travail. It never occurred to me to go out into a hallway or into the ladies' room. This was suggested to me at a later time. I asked God for a second chance, and in His mercy He gave me that second chance. A few days later I was at a home Bible study when the same woman was brought into the house. At once I felt the presence of God and the travail coming forth. I asked one of the leaders if I could release it, and she gave me permission.

Travail is often God making a way. Just as labor in the natural opens the birth canal for the child to be born, travail in the Spirit is God making a way in someones circumstances. Something is birthed into the person's life. Of course this can apply to a ministry, a state, a nation, etc. Even though a person in travail is weeping, it is an experience of tremendous satisfaction. The travail is brought about by the Holy Spirit, and His power and presence bring "fulness of joy" (Psalm 16:11).

If I weep in the natural, my eyes get puffy. I may get a headache and feel drained, but weeping in the Spirit never does that. Sometimes, especially during very deep travail, there is such an awareness of and in some way a partaking of what is in God's heart. He is truly longsuffering.

From the time I received travail at the Aglow meeting, I consistently experienced intercession at church and at Aglow meetings during praise and worship. I had learned to go into a hallway or corner somewhere so as not to disturb anyone when releasing the travail. Eventually there was a prayer room at church to go into when the intercession came forth.

CHAPTER 4

A NEW GIFT—THE HOLY LAUGHTER

One day I spoke on the phone to a friend who lives in Jacksonville. She suggested I come up there as Rodney Howard Brown was ministering and people were receiving the holy laughter. This is laughter brought about by the Holy Spirit. However, it was not possible for me to travel to, Jacksonville at that time. I explained that I couldn't come there, but I believed that if the Lord wanted me to receive the laughter He would give it to me right where I was. Shortly after our conversation, that is exactly what happened.

From that time on I usually received the laughter after the travail. I later learned that the laughter meant that God's purpose had been accomplished and that the victory had been won. It can also mean that the answer is on the way or that the enemy's plan has been averted. Again the Lord confirmed with scripture. In PSALM 2:4 (NEW KING JAMES VERSION) we read: "He who sits in the heavens shall laugh." PSALM 37:12–13 (NKJV) also exclaims, "The wicked plots against the just, and gnashes at him with his teeth. The Lord laughs at him, for He sees that his day is coming." PSALM 59:7–8 declares, "Behold, they belch out with their mouth: swords are in their lips: for who, say they, doth hear? But thou, O Lord, shalt laugh at them, thou shalt have all the heathen in derision."

A remarkable experience regarding the holy laughter happened at an Aglow meeting. Before the meeting the speaker, the leaders, and the prayer team gathered in a circle to pray for the meeting and for the speaker. During the prayers I received very strong intercession for the speaker with travail and birthing (which I will speak of later). God was doing something very powerful and touched her very deeply. After our prayers I saw her off by herself weeping. I knew a work of the Spirit was in progress. After she spoke and women came up for prayer, the speaker directed me to pray for a particular lady. As I prayed for her, I began to receive the holy laughter. This laughter was indeed powerful. I could feel immense power as the laughter came forth and grew louder and louder. Knowing it was by the Holy Spirit, I released it even though it had become so loud everyone in the room could hear it. I had to learn to obey the Holy Spirit and not be concerned with what people thought.

After the intercession lifted and the prayers were finished, I sat down. The woman I prayed for came over to me and revealed that she had been planning to take her life but was delivered. She was set free of the spirit of suicide. Then I understood why there was so much power and volume in the laughter. She was set free! How I stand in awe of God!

I remember quite vividly another experience I had with the holy laughter and an important lesson I learned. This occurred at a women's meeting at church called "The Women of Promise." The teacher, Lois Grider, was a very dear friend and sister in the Lord. Within a year or so of moving to Florida, Lois and I met at the home of a mutual friend for a prayer meeting. Thus began a friendship that continues to this day. Lois is very skilled in teaching and counselling and is a gentle, caring woman of God..

I was talking with a friend before the meeting started when all of a sudden I began to receive the laughter. Lois had begun to speak and was holding up a book entitled *You Can Change Your Destiny.* While she spoke the laughter kept coming but Lois had no way of knowing that it was the holy laughter. I felt I was being rude as she was trying to conduct the class even though I knew that the Holy Spirit was bringing forth the laughter. Nevertheless, I made a mistake and quenched the laughter, thus quenching the Holy Spirit. As I have already said, I had to learn to obey the Holy Spirit and not be concerned about what anybody thought or to lean on my own understanding. This has been a learning experience all along the way.

When I returned home after the meeting, I immediately prayed about what had happened. I said, "Father, I know you are a God of order." Before I could say anything else, God thundered back adamantly, "Yes, but it's MY order!" That was the fastest answer to prayer I ever had, and somewhat of a chastisement.

I discussed the experience with Lois regarding the holy laughter and God's answer to my prayer about His order. She related that as the women shared that evening, there was much depression and sadness. We realized the Lord was desiring to bring His joy as the laughter came forth in the order He chose. So we decided to let the Spirit lead the meetings, and we were all blessed by yielding to God's order. We reaped the blessing at our next meeting when I felt the presence of God and knew that we were supposed to be silent and wait on the Lord. We stood in a circle holding hands, waiting in absolute silence. Suddenly we all felt God's presence and saw what looked like a fog rolling in which had a whitish, yellowish glow. I knew it was God's Shekinah glory. We were all basking in God's glorious presence. Yes, I stand in awe of God!

CHAPTER 5

TWO MORE GIFTS:
THE HOLY SILENCE AND
SONGS OF WORSHIP

From the beginning this has been an amazing
learning experience. Through the years the gifts
of intercession were developed and expanded, and I
was about to receive another. One day as I was on
the floor in our family room in heavy travail, the
travail suddenly stopped. I heard the words from
Revelation 8:1b, "There was silence in heaven about
the space of half an hour." With this came what I call
the holy silence.

I did not fidget nor move at all, but was kept by
the power of the Holy Spirit in complete stillness.
This was not a silence in which I decided to be quiet,

but a powerful silence which held me absolutely still for a length of time. I felt as though I was frozen, so to speak, breathlessly waiting for something to happen. It seemed to me that God was doing something during this stillness, but I did not know what. Through this I learned that sitting silent before the Lord is an important and powerful aspect of prayer. As it is written in PSALM 46:10A, "Be still, and know that I am God." When one enters into the holy presence of God, the majesty and power of His being holds one in silent ecstasy. "But the Lord is in his holy temple: let all the earth keep silence before him" (HABAKKUK 2:20). The prophet Zechariah declared, "Be silent, O all flesh, before the Lord: for he is raised up out of his holy habitation" (ZECHARIAH 2:13).

Ever since the gift of holy silence was imparted, the frequent order of intercession was travail, holy silence, and then laughter. Soon another gift was added. Following the laughter, the Holy Spirit began to quicken songs of worship and praise to me. As I sang the songs given to me by the Holy Spirit, the time of intercession concluded with worship and rejoicing in what the Lord had accomplished.

I pondered all these things and prayed that someday when the Lord takes me home, He will show me all that He did in those times of intercession.

CHAPTER 6

SPIRITUAL BIRTHING

In the fall of 1997, shortly after I started the School of Ministry at our church, an extraordinary event occurred. My husband and I were attending the prayer group that met at church every Sunday morning before the services. On one of these mornings during prayer, the familiar presence of the Holy Spirit came upon me, however, in a different way than ever before.

I felt compelled to get on the floor quickly, not on my face as when in travail, but more on my back in a sort of sitting position with an irresistible urge to push. It was very powerful. I did not understand what was happening but yielded to the work of the Holy Spirit. I experienced a type of breathing that caused power to flow through my body and out of my belly. It is analogous to a woman in labor in the natural. Here the body takes over and the mother-to-be is carried along by the natural physical forces at work in the body's contractions. In the spiritual birthing, the power originates from the Holy Spirit and births something from the spirit realm to the natural realm. Then I heard the pastor in charge of the prayer group whisper, "Oh, Lord, you are birthing something."

I was soon to learn what was being birthed in the prayer room. In the service the pastor announced that the associate pastor was going to start a new church, and this new church was birthed in the Spirit. All glory to God!

One time in the prayer room at church, a birthing was brought forth of tremendous magnitude. In the natural it would have been like delivering a very large baby. I knew it was something huge as I groaned and pushed in heavy "labor." Later the Holy Spirit revealed to me that it was of global significance. Over the years I have had other birthings of global impact.

I always sat in the last row in the sanctuary so that I could leave quickly when the intercession came upon me. One Sunday I was on my way to the prayer room in travail when I heard the words "Galatians 4:19." Needless to say, I looked up the scripture as soon as I came home from church. It reads, "I travail in birth again until Christ be formed in you." Again the Lord had given me scripture to confirm what He was doing. It was thrilling to realize that Paul was a travailer. Paul tells us in Colossians 1:27 that Christ in us is the hope of glory and in Romans 8:29 that we are predestined to be conformed to the image of God's Son.

In 1 Corinthians 3:6 Paul writes, "I have planted, Apollos watered; but God gave the increase." Then in Romans 8:27 (NKJV) Paul explains that "He who searches the hearts knows what the mind of the Spirit is, because He makes intercession for the saints according to the will of God." So in the travail Paul spoke of in Galatians 4:19, the Holy Spirit makes intercession that births Christ in us that we may come to that place of a perfect or mature man, "unto the measure of the stature of the fulness of Christ." (Ephesians 4:13b) When Christ is fully formed within us, we shall walk as He did on the earth.

There were many occasions when I received Galatians 4:19 on the way to the prayer room.

CHAPTER 7

THE GIFT OF VISIONS

In addition to travail, birthing, holy laughter, the holy silence, and worship songs brought forth by the Holy Spirit ,another gift was added, that of visions. I was very touched one Sunday morning at church as we were worshipping the Lord Jesus Christ.

Many in the congregation had their hands raised in worship (1 TIMOTHY 2:8) when I had a vision of the Lord sitting on His throne. The church ceiling seemed to become the floor of heaven, and the hands came up through it. The Lord leaned forward and looked at all the hands with delight. Then He got up and walked among all the raised hands, touching each one, blessing and receiving the worship.

Another time, I saw a hand holding a scalpel about to make an incision and I heard the words, "rightly dividing the Word of God." These words were for our pastor. I also received HEBREWS 4:12. The vision of the hand holding the scalpel ready to divide the flesh is illustrative of this scripture, "For the word of God is quick, and powerful, and sharper than any twoedged sword, piercing even to the dividing asunder of soul and spirit, and of the joints and marrow, and is a discerner of the thoughts and intents of the heart."

I recall a lovely vision I had in church at the start of praise and worship. I saw a heavenly choir enter in single file and go to their seats. They came in at the front of the sanctuary and proceeded to rows of seats along the left side of the sanctuary above the congregation. Words cannot describe the beauty of this heavenly choir. Through visions I learned to appreciate that there is much taking place in the spirit realm during our church services.

Once at a Wednesday evening service I saw "rain" coming down and I felt a strong urge to look upward and smile, which I did. Then much to my amazement and delight, the worship leader said that we should all look toward heaven and smile. God was reigning on us.

Sometimes visions illustrate a scripture such as the one of the hand holding the scalpel. Another was a vision of the Lord seated on His throne. To His side were rows of seats in which the congregation sat. The scripture given to me was EPHESIANS 2:6 (NKJV), "And raised us up together, and made us sit together in the heavenly places in Christ Jesus." Through our union with Him we are seated with Him.

Recently as I was in prayer I began to receive intercession. I saw what looked like a huge white cloud come rolling in and form a platform like surface. Then I saw the Lord standing on it and throwing a lightning bolt down toward Earth. I had never seen a vision like that before and wondered what it meant. A few days later as I was in the Word, I was directed to PSALM 97:4, "His lightnings enlightened the world: the earth saw, and trembled." It is always exciting to receive confirmation from the Lord. God is so real!

CHAPTER 8

LISA'S ACCIDENT

In October of 1994 my daughter Lisa fell off of a runaway horse and somehow landed underneath him on her back. Her horse could not avoid her and stepped on her chest. She had six broken ribs and a collapsed lung, plus damage to the muscles and ligaments of her back.

She lives in Wisconsin and I live in Florida, so when I received this distressing news, I called the hospital to inquire about her condition. They put the call in to her room and she answered the phone but could not talk because she was in too much pain. As I hung up the phone, I felt so much anguish for her that I covered my face with my hands and began to cry. Instantly the Holy Spirit took over and brought forth very heavy travail. Because the presence of God is so strong during travail, I always lay on the floor prostrate on my face before Him. I don't know how long I was on the living room floor in heavy travail. My whole being was absorbed in this powerful intercession, and I knew that God had begun to intervene on her behalf. After quite a while, I had a vision of the Lord seated on His throne next to the Father. I saw the Lord slowly stand up, and He appeared so tall it seemed as though He was as big as the Empire State Building.

Even today, I can see that image of the Lord as if I were looking at a photograph. He arose so majestically from His throne and seemed to tower over the whole earth. As I contemplate it now, I believe He was expressing to me that He is a big God, more than big enough to take care of my daughter. He also transcends all spatial limitations, as He is omnipresent. He connected our spirits in Him, for "we live and move and have our being" in Him (Acts 17:28a).

After the vision I noticed my dog standing at the door, so I got up and took him out for a walk. The anointing was still very strong, so as I walked down to the street corner, I continued to intercede for my daughter and pray in the Spirit.

In the evening, walking my dog was a special time of communing with the Lord. At that time we lived in an area where the lots were from an acre to five acres. Ours was two and a quarter acres, and all were to some degree wooded. The houses were set back away from the road. As we meandered along the grassy side of the road, I enjoyed the beauty of nature and the peaceful atmosphere. But that night was like no other as I cried out earnestly to God on behalf of my daughter under the strong anointing of intercession. Without Him we can do nothing, but we can do all things through Christ who strengthens us. I prayed every healing scripture I could think of, as God promises to watch over His Word to perform it, and that His Word will not return to Him void but will accomplish His purpose.

As I approached our driveway I could feel the holy laughter coming very strong. It was late at night, around eleven o'clock and I didn't want to release it outside as sound carries at night and I knew it would be loud. So I ran to the house and just as I got in the door, it came like a torrent from my innermost being with tremendous power. It was very loud and very mighty and lasted a long time.

If the neighbors could have heard me, they would have thought I was drunk as I howled with laughter. Well, I was drunk, drunk in the Spirit. My whole being tingled with knowing that even though Lisa had an ordeal to endure, she would be all right. I knew the hand of God was upon her. What a powerful divine intervention!

As I write this, I am reminded of the powerful laughter I received for the woman at the Aglow meeting who was delivered from a spirit of suicide. Laughter indicates a positive outcome, as I mentioned in the section on holy laughter. These two instances were the loudest and most powerful that I ever received. After all this, I could still feel the anointing, so I called my friend Kris. Kris and I have been friends and prayer partners for years, and we often prayed together on the phone in the late hours.

Being a good friend of the family and knowing Lisa, her prayers of great compassion were powerful. By then it was about one in the morning and I went to bed!

Amazingly it was still there when I awoke in the morning. The Holy Spirit ushered me into the living room and quickened the song to me, "When the Spirit of the Lord moves upon my heart, I will praise like David praised." He gave me all the verses as I sang and danced in thanksgiving and worship to the Lord. When the Holy Spirit quickens a song to me, I don't have to think about or search my memory for the words. They just flow through my mouth effortlessly.

The intercession had lasted so long the night before that He gave me the song and worship portion in the morning. He gives His beloved sleep. I can't remember how long I was singing and dancing before the Lord, but the anointing was still there when I went to the Bible study in the afternoon.

Lisa was in the hospital for a week. A nurse told her she had the mark of a hoof on her chest, which eventually faded. Her brother Mark, who worked as a computer consultant for the University of Illinois at Urbana, took vacation time to step to her side. He took her home from the hospital and took care of her. She was completely healed and in five months was able to ride again. Her passion for horses and riding continues as she and her horse work diligently to advance in dressage training.

CHAPTER 9

WATERWAYS

In October of 1999, I was introduced to Patty Cushman by a mutual friend. We all attended the same church. Knowing I'm an intercessor, she invited me to come to her house to pray, which I did. On the day that we met for prayer, I told her that I was not worthy to pray. I had become involved in a situation that I should not have been in, and I needed to repent. According to 1 JOHN 1:9, "If we confess our sins, he is faithful and just to forgive us our sins and to cleanse us from all unrighteousness." As I confessed my sin to God and repented, she also began to repent. There must have been a spirit of repentance, because we both continued in confession and repentance with a broken and contrite spirit before the Lord.

At one point I lamented that I felt like a broken vessel, as David bemoaned in PSALM 31:12. Suddenly an astounding thing happened. I saw water coming into the room under one of the doors. This was not physical water but spiritual water. The water came in so rapidly that there were little waves and foam on the water. I stared in utter amazement as I exclaimed to Patty what was happening. She said she wished she could see it too, so I laid my hand on her head and prayed for the gift of visions. Shortly after that she received a vision of two hands setting down two new pots filled with water. Though I felt like a broken vessel, through repentance God brought restoration and filled us both with living water.

When the water became about a foot deep, I sensed that we were to lay down in it because it was a manifestation of God's restoring, healing, living water. As we both lay in this miraculous water, we thrilled with the supernatural demonstration that came in response to our heartfelt repentance. This experience also impressed upon me the tremendous power of repentance. Later that night after I had gone home, I received a phone call from Patty. Being a gifted artist, Patty had recently purchased an eight-by-ten-foot canvas from Home Depot. Her husband made a frame for it, and there it sat for three weeks. Patty wasn't really sure what she was going to paint on it, but God knew.

After I left, she painted the vision of the hands setting down the two pots filled with water on the canvas. We were both so excited about the painting and how God had her prepare the canvas ahead of time.

Again the Lord gave me a confirming scripture in HEBREWS 10:22, "Let us draw near with a true heart in full assurance of faith, having our hearts sprinkled from an evil conscience, and our bodies washed with pure water." That was the beginning of our weekly meetings. We put on worship music and sat silently before the Lord. Soon we were in His presence, and intercession was brought forth by the Holy Spirit.

The second time we met, as we entered into the presence of the Lord, I had a vision of a huge waterfall and heard the words "Victoria Falls." Patty looked it up and found out that it is the largest curtain of water in the world. Being that it is in Africa, Patty queried, "Am I supposed to go to Africa?" I chuckled. The Holy Spirit revealed that the vision represented the magnitude of what the Lord was doing in the ministry that began in the water of cleansing. The waterfall was the second thing Patty painted on the big canvas.

As our intercession proceeded, more was added to the canvas until it was eventually filled. In her prayer time the Lord disclosed that the name of the ministry He had established was to be Waterways. Another vision I had as we were before the Lord was of a hand holding a pitcher of water about to be poured out. The color of the pitcher was a dark cobalt blue. I shall refer to this vision again.

Patty painted a beautiful mural on one wall of the study. It pictured a young woman sitting on a beautiful veranda with plants decorating it. She included her dog, Sid, in the painting. Sid had recently been put down due to age and illness. In one corner of the painting stood a lovely pink vase.

One day when Patty and I were before the Lord in His presence, I felt impressed to lie in the water.

As soon as I laid my head on the floor, I felt a dog licking my face. I asked the Lord if it was Sid, and He gave me laughter, which meant yes. Then I saw myself sitting on that veranda at the top of the stairs leading up to it, and next to me sat the Lord. He was leaning casually against the post that extended from the floor to the ceiling. Down the stairway and a short distance from it was the shore of the sea. Suddenly a huge, dark wave of water was coming toward us. The Lord said, "All I have to do is say 'peace,'" and the wave instantly disappeared.

Then another wave, light blue in color, rose up and came toward us. I sensed it was benevolent, and it washed over me giving me, peace. Then I came back to the floor of the study. Patty's cat had kittens and she was preoccupied with them and had not lain down in the water. I excitedly related to Patty that I had been in the mural and Sid licked my face. I explained about the Lord being there, the waves, and what He said. Months later, when others were coming to our meetings, a dear sister in the Lord brought a beautiful vase and told me that the Lord instructed her to give it to me. She even argued with Him, saying that I like blue better, but the Lord insisted. The vase was pink. I was flabbergasted. Before the others started coming to our meetings, the room was rearranged and a chair was in front of the part of the mural where that vase was painted. So she had never seen it.

When she handed me the vase my heart leaped for joy, because I knew the Lord was confirming all that happened when I was on the veranda with Him. I hurried to move the chair and show her that the vase the Lord instructed her to give me was identical to the one painted in the mural that had been covered from view by the chair. We all marveled and praised the Lord.

Patty and I met once a week for four months before others joined our meetings. Each time we put on worship music and waited quietly upon the Lord. As we came into His presence, intercession was brought forth by the power of the Holy Spirit. When I say "intercession," this includes travail, birthing, silence, visions, and all that I have heretofore explained. I do not know how to describe the power I feel in my body as the Holy Spirit does these works. Most of the time I experience heat around my face and body. Sometimes the power is so intense that I need help. I was very blessed for many years to have Martha Murillo's help during times of intercession at church, at Aglow, and at Waterways.

The person who does this is referred to as a midwife as in birthing in the natural. At church she would place her hand on my back as the power was flowing through my body, and she said it felt like electricity was moving through my back. I could feel the power flow into me and out again to the congregation. Often at Aglow meetings I would go into a corner to release the intercession, and she was always there to help me. She herself is a mighty prayer warrior, pure of heart and fervent in prayer

I remember so clearly the last time Patty and I met by ourselves. We went before the Lord in our usual way, but this day we were lifted up into the spirit realm, enraptured in His presence. We sat in utter silence for what seemed like a very short while. Then I saw a golden waterfall. It looked like liquid gold pouring down with glittery, golden globules splashing from the golden flow. The gold speaks of the glory of God. We looked at each other with eyes big as saucers as if to say, "Did you see that?"

As it turns out, we did. As we each excitedly shared what we had seen, we discovered that we both had received the same identical vision. We were absolutely giddy with joy and amazement. Then we looked at the clock and found that four hours had passed while we were before the Lord. It seemed like minutes! Talk about a grand finale; this was spectacular! In our elation we praised and magnified the Lord.

Naturally our enthusiasm for what the Lord was doing in our meetings was shared with our friends, resulting in others joining us. One day a dear sister came to the door with a blue pitcher exactly like the one I saw in the vision of the hand holding the pitcher about to pour the water out. She knew nothing of the vision. The Lord had instructed her to give it to us. It was just awesome the way the Lord confirmed.

CHAPTER 10

THE VISION OF THE LORD'S ROBES

Eight of us were assembled in the study at Patty's house to seek the Lord's face. Patty opened with prayer. Travail came quickly to me. The first vision I had was of a cross with a wreath of flowers around the middle where the two beams intersected. I heard the words, "Embrace the cross." Then I heard by the Spirit, "Come to Me, all you who labor and are heavy laden, and I will give you rest" (MATTHEW 11:28 NKJV). Next I heard, "In the world you will have tribulation; but be of good cheer, I have overcome the world" (JOHN 16:33B NKJV). I then heard the song "I have decided to follow Jesus," and I sang it.

After that the Lord said we did not choose Him, He chose us. This is found in JOHN 15:16. This was followed by a curious vision in which I saw the lower part of the Lord's robes and His staff. My attention was drawn to the fullness of His robes. His cloak was beige and the robe was off-white. I kept marveling at how unusually full His robes were. It reminded me of the full skirts we wore when I was in high school in the fifties. In order to expand the outward flow of the full skirt, we wore special slips. I could not take my eyes off of how very full His robes were. The presence of God was so strong and I heard, "I am making My face to shine upon you," (referring to NUMBERS 6:25) followed by "Stretch out your stakes and enlarge your tents," (referring to ISAIAH 54:2).

Our meeting was held on Wednesday. The following Monday night, after I went to bed, I strongly felt God's presence. Then I heard, "For in him dwelleth all the fulness of the Godhead bodily." I knew the scripture was in COLOSSIANS 2:9 and that God had just told me what the fullness of the robes meant in the vision. I was intoxicated with the joy of the Lord for revealing the meaning of the vision and again confirming His word. Wow God!

During the time when the Holy Spirit is bringing forth travail and intercession my eyes are closed so that I can concentrate on what the Spirit is showing me and telling me. The other members of the group are in an attitude of worship praying in the Spirit. Some are on their knees and others lay prostrate on the floor before the Lord. I have always found that the power of God is amplified by the others praying in agreement with what the Spirit is doing.

CHAPTER 11

WATER INTO WINE

One day as I was driving to Patty's house for our weekly meeting, I began to receive travail in my car before I arrived at Patty's house. The power that I experience upon and in my body when I receive intercession was upon me, bringing forth weeping. I have had travail a few times while driving and wondered if angels are helping me drive at those times.

I reached Patty's house, and as I came down the driveway I saw Patty standing outside near the driveway. Her house is a European style with the buildings in a u shape around the pool. On one side is a two-story structure with the living room, dining room, kitchen, and laundry room on the first floor, and the bedrooms on the second floor. Another structure facing the driveway is the study where we had our meetings. Another structure to the side and back of the study faces the pool as the two-story structure does. A sidewalk goes to the house on the right and another sidewalk makes a left turn to go to the study.

As I approached Patty, I was so in the Spirit with travail, I could only say that we needed to pray. We hastened into the study on the left. I was already receiving intercession when Patty put the worship music on. The Spirit drew me deeper into powerful travail. I felt that I had been transported to a heavenly realm. My whole being was bathed in His holy presence for I don't know how long.

I saw a golden censor. Then I saw the Lord and the pots filled with water and watched as the Lord was turning the water into wine. It was like watching a video. There was such a presence of the Lord and His power. We were all transported into the spirit realm. During this time the Spirit would direct Patty and I in ministry to those present.

When the Spirit lifted, Patty called me to come outside. As I came out the door, the house was across from me. When I approached the house, Patty directed me to look up, and there on the side of the house above eye level she had painted a mural of the Lord changing the water into wine. I was so overtaken with awe of the Lord and amazement. Patty had painted the mural the day before, and I did not see it when I got to her house because the travail was so strong.

As I contemplate this awesome experience I realize that God had everything all planned perfectly. Patty was led to paint the mural of Jesus turning the water into wine on her house the day before we met. I was given travail before I arrived so we went directly and quickly into the study. I did not go near the house on our right, so did not see the painting. During the intercession I was taken into the spirit realm and given the vision of the Lord changing the water into wine. God confirmed His Word in such a beautiful way and in perfect detail. As I reflect on this, I believe that God's plan for our lives is also worked out in perfect detail according to His will. This realization filled me with peace.

CHAPTER 12

WATERWAYS MEETING

MAY 31, 2000

During the almost two years of our Waterways meetings, we felt that we were back in the book of Acts because of the many supernatural occurrences. This day held an amazing one.

Six of us met that day. We began with worship. The presence of God came and I felt the Holy Spirit put my hand in the position for the anointing of the water. I felt something coming out of my right hand. Oftentimes when I am receiving intercession the Spirit puts my hands in different positions. I felt great power flowing through my hands. Once at an Aglow meeting my dear friend and sister in Christ, who is a seer, saw a tree of life coming out of my hand. I could feel it but could not see it.

This day I felt something coming out of my right hand, and after a while I felt I should go to each person and release the power on them. I went first to one, then another, who began to weep. Birthing came forth for her. Then I went to Patty, and she went down under the power. As I went to another, much intercession and travail came forth for her.

Patty came over and stood behind her, which was good as she started falling in the Spirit. She said that she wanted to be baptized again. After the others left, this sister came back to be baptized in Patty's pool. Just the three of us were there. Patty did not want to get wet, so I went into the pool with the one wanting to be baptized to hold her as Patty prayed in the Spirit on the pool deck. The one being baptized went under by the Spirit three times. I did not put her under; I just held on to her and pulled her up each time she went down. Then something happened I will never forget.

I saw Patty flying from the deck where she was behind us and right past us into the pool. She did not jump. The Spirit flew her in. Our mouths dropped open in utter shock. There was Patty soaking wet in the pool; she didn't want to get wet, but the Spirit literally picked her up and flew her in. She was horizontal as she passed us. We just stood there in disbelief, but we saw it with our own eyes. We were so excited at what had just happened and began to laugh about how Patty was intent on not going in the pool, yet there she was. I said we would have to call her the flying nun. There was a television series years ago, called, *The flying Nun*. Sally Field played the part of the flying nun. God is holy, but He has a great sense of humor too.

CHAPTER 13

PRAYER MEETING AT
SISTER JEANNE'S

OCTOBER 28, 2009

We met at sister Jeanne's house for our weekly
Aglow prayer and Bible study. In attendance
was our president, Karen, her mother, Margaret,
Linda, Farhat, Cary, Anna, Jeanne, and myself. I was
a little late, and when I arrived Karen told me they
were praying for one of our sisters who was very ill.
Her blood sugar was dangerously high at 471. She
could have gone into a coma or worse. We all prayed
for her, and then Jeanne took her to the hospital.

We continued in prayer, each one praying as the
Spirit led. The Spirit quickened the chorus of a song
based on ZECHARIAH 4:6 that I frequently receive during
intercession. It goes as follows: "It's not by might, it's

not by power, but it is by my Spirit, saith the Lord, and this mountain, this mountain shall be removed, and I will build my temple in you and what I promise I will do. But it's not by might, it's not by power, but it is by my Spirit, saith the Lord."

Cary, who is our praise and worship leader, beautifully sang Psalm 27. Then I strongly felt we were to enter into worship, so Karen put on worship music. As we were worshipping, the power of intercession came forth and I began to receive travail. I got up from my chair and without thinking, being led by the Spirit, I went down on the floor on my face before the Lord. This in itself was a miracle as I was not able to do this for eight years due to a physical condition. Lying on the floor before the Lord as the travail and birthing were released, I saw the Lord's feet and the hem of His white robe right in front of me. The holy silence came after the travail and birthing, while my gaze remained on the vision in front of me. When the Spirit lifted, I got up and went to my chair. My eyes were closed as I sat in rapt attention to the beautiful presence of the Lord. Then I saw the Lord standing in the middle of the room.

Around His head where the crown of thorns had once so cruelly pressed, I saw a garland of flowers. He held out His hands, palms up. I sensed I should get up and put my hands palm down on His hands. I prayed for confirmation as I usually do, because I do not want anything of my own flesh or imagination to defile the work of the Spirit. As I waited for confirmation, I heard the Lord saying that He had called us, appointed us, anointed us and was drawing us into a deeper level of His Spirit. I kept hearing the word "come," so I did get up and go to Him and placed my hands on His.

Immediately I felt power flow through my body. I knew the Lord wanted everyone to do this. When one is touched by the Lord so strongly, weeping comes, and through my sobs I related to the others what I had seen and what the Lord desired of everyone.

Linda got up and put her hands on His, and the power of God came on her mightily. She, also, knew that His presence was there. Cary was next to get up and put her hands on His. She went down on the floor under the power of God. Then Karen put her hands on His and took the blessing to her mother and to Anna. She received a beautiful word from the Lord for her mother. Each of them by faith put their hands on the Lord's hands as they had not seen the vision.

As Karen stood before the Lord, I heard the words that our faith was pleasing to Him. When the ministry by the Spirit ended, we closed in prayer. Over two hours had passed.

Later that evening a phone call revealed that our prayers were answered. Our sister who was taken to the hospital was put in the hands of a new physician, given new medication, and her condition was being monitored and controlled. She was also directed to take a class to be instructed in her diet.

This is a miracle. Miracles happen around us every day if we open our eyes to see them and to see that the Lord is guiding and protecting us.

Our intercession brought forth much fruit and blessing to us all, and our sister received a new path to benefit her health. As I contemplate the happenings of this day, two scriptures come to mind: MATTHEW 18:19–20 (NKJV) states that "if two of you agree on earth concerning anything that they ask, it will be done for them by My Father in heaven. For where two or three are gathered together in My name, I am there in the midst of them." And in JAMES 5:16B (NKJV) we read that "the effective, fervent prayer of a righteous man avails much."

CHAPTER 14

SKY ANGEL

It was at an Aglow meeting in 1987 that I first heard about Sky Angel Christian television, then known as Dominion DBS. Jeanine Johnson and Dayna Meserve were the speakers. Jeanine Johnson is the wife of the founder of Sky Angel, Mr. Robert Johnson. She spoke on how the Lord had called her husband to establish this monumental undertaking and confirmed to her that it was a calling of God. I was very intrigued as she related how the Lord's hand directed the path of their lives into this new direction. Prior to devoting his life to this awesome task, Mr. Johnson had had a very successful marketing and research business in Michigan.

Then Dayna, who was Mr. Johnson's assistant, spoke on the progress of the project and the efforts being made to inform the church and raise support.

I immediately had a witness in my spirit that this was an important work of God. I made some inquiries and learned that I could become involved by being a volunteer, which I did. I also worked there for a season and then continued on as a volunteer with many others until volunteers were no longer needed. My husband and I were enthusiastic supporters of this vision for Christian programming and were so thrilled when Sky Angel began broadcasting multiple television and radio stations.

In order to get this project up and running, many very difficult challenges were faced. It was an uphill battle, and Mr. Johnson worked tirelessly and made many sacrifices to fulfill his calling to bring Sky Angel into being.

While I was there I worked with Louise Melin, who became Mr. Johnson's assistant after Dayna left to pursue her nursing career. Louise was also the office manager until her retirement. In addition to being very capable, efficient, and organized, she was a gifted humorist, which made working with her an absolute joy. I treasure the memories of those days.

On June 8, 2001, I went to lunch with Jeanine Johnson, Louise Melin, and several others on staff at Sky Angel. After lunch we went back to the office for a little visit, but the Holy Spirit had something else in mind. On the table in the conference room was the architect's model for a new center to be built. As Louise was explaining it to me, I began to feel the presence of the Holy Spirit very strongly as He brought forth intercession for this great work. I received very strong travail and birthing. As the tears of intercession were flowing, I was impressed to wash Jeanine's feet with the tears. I remembered that an intercessor once told me that the Lord showed her that the tears were the anointing. The tears were not mine but God's, and I washed her feet with the tears flowing from my eyes. I felt so strongly that the Lord was expressing His love for the Johnsons and that He was pleased with their obedience, sacrifices, and perseverance in bringing Sky Angel to pass.

Then I turned to Louise, as I felt that God had a blessing for her, and by the power of the Holy Spirit intercession came forth, and something was birthed in the Spirit for her.

Interestingly, not long before this occasion, one of the members of Sky Angel's staff was at one of our Waterways prayer meetings. During our prayers the Holy Spirit brought forth a very powerful birthing. The Spirit impressed upon me that it dealt with the global vision of Sky Angel.

CHAPTER 15

A DIVINE APPOINTMENT

A week or so before our February 2010 Aglow outreach meeting, the Lord reminded me of a Wednesday evening church service sometime in the late 1990s. I was sitting in the last row as I always did so that I could leave quickly to go to the prayer room to release travail. This night, as praise and worship proceeded, I was receiving very powerful intercession. On this occasion, Martha was not with me as the strong intercession came forth. Suddenly I heard the familiar voice of Sheila Zellers standing behind the last row, praying.

I met Sheila at Aglow in 1987, the year my late husband and I moved to Naples. I was blessed by Aglow in Wisconsin and was happy to connect with the Aglow in Naples.

Sheila became president in 1987 and served as president until 1992. She taught Aglow Bible studies at her home and taught Bible studies at church. She also founded night Aglow in 1993 and was president until the latter part of 1996. She helped pioneer a church in Naples starting in 1992 through 1994. She is a gifted vocalist, recording artist and composer.

That night as I heard Sheila praying behind me, I got up and asked her if she would help me. She agreed. As the power of the intercession (comparable to labor pains in intensity) continued, I held on to Sheila, as it was so strong I could not stand up without her help. While these powerful waves of intercession, birthings, and God's creative energies were being released, Sheila continued praying for the church. I knew from the previous huge birthing that I had experienced in the prayer room that these were of global significance.

I had always thought that the intercession I received that night was for the church, but what the Lord revealed to me a week or so before our February 2010 meeting was that it was for Sheila.

It is so amazing how the Lord arranges events for His kingdom purpose. I did not know Sheila would be at the February Aglow meeting but God did. After the speaker gave her message, she ministered to the people in the gifts of the Spirit. During this time she prophesied over Sheila. With the recent revelation that the intercession brought forth over a decade ago was for Sheila, I very much witnessed to the words spoken over Sheila. Afterwards Sheila and I were talking, and I expressed this to her. I asked her if she remembered the time we prayed together at church. She did remember, and I shared with her that the Lord has recently revealed to me that the intercession I received that night was for her. As we spoke about it ,I knew I was supposed to put it in the book.

Then about a week after the Aglow meeting, I awoke one morning at four o'clock. The presence of the Lord was so strong and there was such a sweet fellowship with Him. I spoke no words, nor were any necessary, as I lay bathed in His presence. At the end of this time of communion with Him, He showed me a vision that I had years ago while Sheila was president of Aglow. I remembered it very well. In the vision I saw a very dry, sandy wasteland. In the foreground was a large well filled with pure, clean water. Then I saw the desert filled with people who looked like they were starving. They were, in fact, starving for the life-giving, soul-saving Word of God. Then I saw Sheila dip a big ladle into the well and take it to the people, indicating she would be taking the Word of God to many peoples and nations.

Since the time of that intercession over a decade ago Sheila has founded her own ministry, Motivated By Love. She was ordained a pastor with the Church of God, Cleveland, Tennessee, in August 2007.

She teaches and preaches with great anointing, as well as moving in the gifts of the Spirit.

I recently learned that Pastor Sheila went from being a credentialed exhorter minister in the Church of God of Cleveland, Tennessee to the highest rank a woman can hold as an ordained minister.

CHAPTER 16

SPENDING TIME
IN INTERCESSION
TOGETHER

I met Sharon Hail at an Aglow meeting in May of 2007. Sharon is a very spirit-filled woman of God with an impressive background. She has a bachelor's degree in education from Arkansas State University and a master's degree from the University of Arkansas. She taught school for thirteen years. She attended Rhema Bible College for three years. At the time I met her she was the secretary of day Aglow and later became the president. We hit it off right away. I received intercession at that meeting which caught Sharon's attention. She is remarkably sensitive to the moving of the Holy Spirit.

We talked after the meeting and made plans to get together. Sharon came to my house and we went before the Lord just as Patty and I did. We put on worship music and waited on the Lord. Soon His mighty presence came upon us. Keep in mind that when I say I received intercession, it is a very powerful work of the Holy Spirit lifting me up in the Spirit.

As the presence of God became stronger, I had an amazing vision. I saw two huge feathered wings. Sharon and I were sitting side by side in two easy chairs. One of the wings was over Sharon and extended from her all the length of the house and past the lawn and out to the street. The other wing covered me and extended from me out to the back of the house past the backyard and all the way to a lake that the houses were built around. My favorite psalm is PSALM 91 and I was seeing verse 4: "He shall cover thee with his feathers, and under his wings shalt thou trust." Those are some mighty big wings!

Then I saw a huge bird that, right before my eyes, morphed into an intercontinental jet. Under each wing there was a seat. Sharon was sitting in one and I in the other. The big bird, like a dove, represented the Holy Spirit, and the jet conveyed to me that our intercession was of a global impact.

Sharon wrote in her notes that she saw "God, the Father, spinning the earth on His finger. We were in His abode. Then He gave us the earth. He literally put it in our hands."

There were occasions during deep and powerful intercession that I was impressed to raise my arms as if I were putting them around the earth. The presence of God at those times was very strong, beyond my ability to describe, but I would know by the magnitude of the power that the intercession was global. At those times it was necessary to "be in pain, and labor to bring forth" (MICAH 4:10A NKJV)

Often I think that one day, when I go to be with Jesus, He will show me the great and mighty things He did during all those times of intercession.

CHAPTER 17

SHARON, A FRIEND OF SHARON'S, AND MYSELF BEFORE THE LORD

JUNE 23, 2007

I put on the music, "The Song of the Angels," and we sat silently before the Lord. Soon we felt the presence of the Holy Spirit, and I began to receive intercession.

The first vision I had was of Sharon riding on the back of a huge, white bird, which I knew represented the Holy Spirit. I could see mountains below. She had on glasses and was holding onto and looking into an appointment book. She wet her thumb on her tongue as she turned the pages in full concentration on her book. She was not distracted at all by her amazing flight in the heavenlies.

Then the Lord appeared as both the Son of God and the son of man. I saw Him from the chest down. His cloak was beautiful velvet the color of scarlet. His robe was a plain beige. The robes were very full. "For in Him dwelleth all the fulness of the Godhead bodily" (COLOSSIANS 2:9).

The intercession and travail came for the nations. I saw what looked like ribbons coming down with ornaments or round globes on the bottom. They kept coming down. I asked the Lord what it was and He said, "Souls." Then I saw a multitude of people followed by hundreds of white doves being released and going every which way. After this I saw a circular waterfall and the three of us were running in the falls like children running through the water from a sprinkler.

At the close of the intercession the Lord was giving me a sword and (I think) a shield. He was putting on me the armor of God. Later I saw a huge sword. It was gold and He told me to take it. At the end He told me to smite the floor with it five times.

When the Spirit departed, we discussed what the Lord had shown us. The vision of Sharon on the big bird indicated she would be going on mission trips in the future. She has already been on mission trips to Ghana and Tanzania in Africa, to Mexico, and to the Navajo Indian reservations in Arizona and Honduras.

CHAPTER 18

SHARON AND I
BEFORE THE LORD

I began to receive intercession as soon as the music began. It came so strong I could not sit down. The Spirit was moving my hands in different ways as it often occurs. At one point my arms were pushing away from my body with much power as I received powerful birthing. In the first vision I saw a fence with multitudes of people behind it. The ones at the front were reaching their arms through the fence. Then I saw Jesus pulling the fences down and the people thronging around Him, thanking Him. He set the captives free.

I sat down, still receiving travail and birthing. Then I felt impressed to get up. As I came to the foyer of my house, I had a vision of two huge columns. They were draped with white curtains. Inside there was a very large banquet hall. The Lord walked toward me dressed in a tuxedo. We had on wedding dresses. It was the marriage supper of the Lamb. Then I saw a huge dome over my head. I could see the stars, and the Lord reached out and grabbed a handful of stars. At the ending I saw a vision of the Lord wearing His Hebrew cloak, and the intercession was very powerful.

Here are notes Sharon made during this time of intercession exactly as she wrote them.

Balls of Gold into Emily's hands
Huge Waterfall
Going deeper into things of God
Depositing in us treasures
Gifts of Spirit to bring forth fruit
Deeper waters

JANUARY 4, 2008

During my prayer time I had a vision of myself in full armor of God, my sword held up, and my foot on the enemy. The scripture I was given was LUKE 10:19, "Behold, I give unto you power to tread on serpents and scorpions, and over all the power of the enemy: and nothing shall by any means hurt you."

Later Sharon Hail came over and we prayed for our leaders, for the economy, for the social structure, and for Aglow. Then we put the music on and waited on the Lord. In the beginning Sharon received travail. I stood next to her, and I was holding the whole earth high as I could reach upwards. Then I was given a mixture of travail, birthing, laughter, and things I do not know how to describe. At one point as I received laughter I heard, "One can flee a thousand, two can flee ten thousand."

I received a sword and hit the ground with it seven or eight times. I saw the Lord standing in the river Jordon. He had His robe held up just above His knees. I bowed down and He anointed me. The water flowed around and upon me. I received an ecstasy of His presence that is indescribable. The vision lasted quite awhile as much intercession, laughter, and travail came forth by the power of the Holy Spirit.

MARCH 19, 2008

The first vision: I saw the Lord. His robe was very, very white. All the attention in the vision was on the robe. The whiteness speaks of Him as the light of the world. It also brings to mind the transfiguration when "his raiment was white as the light" (MATTHEW 17:2).

There were others around Him. I was aware of their presence, but I was not able to see them. Then I saw a red dove, glistening and flying normally. After this I saw an eagle flying downward rapidly as if to catch a prey. This indicated to me the need to be aggressive against the enemy.

There was much travail and birthing with hand movements. I saw a large globe (the earth). My arms went all the way around it. The glory of the Lord shall cover the earth.

I saw water flowing into the room just as it did when Patty and I first prayed together.

CHAPTER 19

SURPRISE

On the evening of November 30, 2009, I received a phone call from a dear sister in the Lord. In the course of our conversation we were discussing different versions of the Bible. I recently received a new version of the Bible and began reading to her from it. As I read I could sense the presence of the Lord.

The more I read, the stronger His presence became. It gradually increased until the power of God was so strong that I could not read anymore. As I have said before, when the Holy Spirit moves, there is great power.

Travail came forth with intermittent songs, birthings, and laughter. It wasn't in a particular order, and there were some things in this intercession that were unlike any that I had before. Powerful intercession was being made according to the will of God.

My dear sister on the phone came under this mighty anointing as well, ,and we were swept away in the presence of the Lord. It must have been an hour or so that we reveled in fellowship with the Lord, basking in His divine presence with pure delight. Words cannot describe the ecstasy of this experience. We were propelled into a heavenly realm.

It was such a lovely surprise. We were not in prayer or worship, but we were reading God's Word, and He came and met us there. I love surprises like this when God moves by His Spirit in an unexpected way. During this time my "sister" received the holy laughter. She had wondered what the holy laughter was like, and in this time in His presence, she received it. What a surprise! She said it was joy beyond measure. In the presence of the Lord there is fullness of joy (PSALM 16:11).

About a week later I received an e-mail from her describing many fabulous blessings that the Lord is doing in her life.

Wow! How great thou art!

CHAPTER 20

NOTES FROM MY JOURNAL

SEPTEMBER 22, 2005

Nancy Swartz and I were praying against Hurricane Rita. I received intercession and a vision. Mighty, huge angels were confronting the hurricane and absorbing the buffeting of the storm. The Holy Spirit led us to pray for Israel, for our leaders, and then showed me the enemy's three towers of deception, ungodliness and unrighteousness.

OCTOBER 5, 2005

There was a strong presence of the Lord. I saw round shafts coming down from above, honey in color, with a thick consistency of oil running down. These shafts of oil seemed to be all over the church. The oil was the charisma, the anointing. Then I saw everyone in the Holy of Holies. My attention was drawn to the curtains covering the top where the *ruach* (breath) of God would cause them to go up and down with His breathing. There was rain coming from heaven. The church roof was covered with gold, and a cloud of gold dust came out from the walls of the church and began to drift outward from the church.

NOVEMBER 17, 2005 AGLOW

Everyone was standing in a circle, and we went around the circle, each one giving a prayer. After I sat down and was interceding, I had a vision of the throne of God. It was covered with gold and around it was a gold hanging with a pattern in it that was a dark or blood red color. It was majestic and holy. I also saw a very large ear, indicating to me that God was listening to our prayers. During praise and worship I saw earphones (Let him who has ears to hear, hear...).

Then I saw a beautiful lamp like the lamp in the story of the ten virgins. It was burning very brightly, and all around it was a very bright glow. As I looked at some of the ladies, they seemed to be the lamp, and all around was a river of fire. Later on as I was thinking about the vision, I heard the words, "Be aglow and burning with the spirit," which is the Aglow motto.

NOVEMBER 26, 2005 RESTORATION CHURCH

As I received intercession, I had a vision of the Lord Jesus Christ entering into church wearing a long cloak that was a deep red velvet, very rich and royal in appearance. On His head where the crown of thorns had been, there was a wreath, like a Christmas wreath of evergreens. The green wreath spoke to me of life, and He is life, "the way, the truth, and the life" (JOHN 14:6A).

CHAPTER 21

THE HOLY HUSH

NIGHT AGLOW JULY 16, 2007

As I arrived at the location of the meeting, I saw signs in the parking lot informing us that the meeting was a "Holy Hush", and we should not speak. As I entered the fellowship hall, I could see that much planning and preparation had been done for the meeting. I immediately felt the presence of God. It was so strong that intercession came at once. I sat down at a table near the door to write down the visions I was receiving. The lighting in the room was a soft glow. No one spoke a word. In the front of the hall there were large pillows upon which people sat or reclined, praying. There were two large canopies or tents decorated with white, lacy curtains. Inside one of them the leaders of night Aglow were washing feet and doing foot massage. Inside the other there were two professional massage therapists, sisters in the Lord, giving massages. One was giving massage on a special massage chair and the other on a massage table. Someone else was giving hand and arm massage with lotion. The leaders, following Christ's example as the servant, were quietly ministering to the women. Some were whispering prayers in the Spirit. Just as Esther was prepared to meet the king, these women were being pampered and prepared to meet the King of kings.

The atmosphere was reverent, holy, and anointed. It took my breath away and permeated my whole being as I sat and wrote the visions I received. First I saw a vessel, then I saw the hand of the Lord with a bullion of gold in it. Then I saw red wine flowing, which spoke to me of communion with the Lord. After writing down the visions, I soaked awhile in the purity and beauty of the atmosphere before going over to the tent where they were washing feet. There were chairs outside where one could wait their turn. When it was my turn, I went in and sat down with my feet in the water. As I was soaking, the night Aglow president came over and washed my feet. She received weeping, and I was so blessed. I thought, " How wonderful, Lord, that she is receiving travail for me." Just then I had a very unusual vision of the Lord. He was standing behind her with His hands on her shoulders. He had on a very white suit. My attention was drawn to the jacket. The shoulders were very wide and extended way out past the body, giving the appearance of huge shoulders. As I marveled at this vision, I heard the words, "And the government shall be upon his shoulder" (ISAIAH 9:6). That explained the appearance of the jacket having such broad shoulders. Wow!

Next my attention was drawn to His head. It seemed most curious to me that He was wearing a turban. As I was engrossed in this most unusual vision of Him, His presence was very powerful, and a very large birthing and intercession came forth.

The next day in my prayer and scripture time I was led to EZEKIEL 24:17 and 23. These two verses both have the word "turban" in them. Although I had read the book of Ezekiel, I did not remember that. Again the Lord was confirming His word to the smallest detail. Regarding the vision of the vessel, I received 2 CORINTHIANS 4:7. "But we have this treasure in earthen vessels, that the excellency of the power may be of God, and not of us."

The vision of the Lord holding the gold bullion in His hand was revealed in 1 PETER 1:7: "That the trial of your faith, being much more precious than of gold that perisheth, though it be tried with fire, might be found unto praise and honour and glory at the appearing of Jesus Christ."

JULY 16, 2009 AGLOW

As our president, Karen Wood, was praying, I had a vision of the Father leaning forward in the throne with His hand up to His ear, inclining His ear to hear the prayers.

AUGUST 13, 2009 AGLOW

During praise and worship I received intercession. There was a strong presence of God. I saw Karen, our president, become as a flame of fire leaping upward. "He makes "His ministers a flame of fire" (PSALM 104:4B NKJV)

I also saw a stairway as a ladder to heaven. Then a cloud overshadowed us and poured down silver rain. Silver speaks of redemption.

Later when we were all in a circle praying, I saw the cloud moving out from the church in all directions. I heard the words, "God is on the move."

APRIL 25, 2009 AGLOW

Upon arriving, I received intercession immediately. There was much travail and birthing. I saw a huge throne. It was empty. Then I saw all of us sitting there as little girls. Then we were being equipped. Yes, we are His children, but He has given us great power and weapons. "(For the weapons of our warfare are not carnal, but mighty through God to the pulling down of strong holds;) Casting down imaginations, and every high thing that exalteth itself against the knowledge of God" (2 CORINTHIANS 10:4–5)

I saw heaven open and what looked like molten gold flow down from heaven and begin to cover the earth. As the liquid gold was coming down from heaven, great power came upon me, and I was holding the earth as God poured His power upon it. My whole body could feel much power. It filled me and poured onto the globe of the earth as my arms were surrounding the planet.

Then as the worship music was playing on a CD, I saw the Lord seated on His throne, and light was emanating from Him. We were literally being bathed in His light. He is the light of the world.

Then I had the same vision that I had at the March Aglow meeting, of the Lord in an ermine robe. At the meeting, during worship, I had a vision of the Lord entering in. He had on a very luxurious full-length coat. At a certain song I began to receive very strong intercession, travail, and birthings. The Lord's coat looked like an ermine robe, thick, soft, and very rich. I asked what it meant, and the answer was that the Lord came to us as El Shaddai, the God of more than enough.

CHAPTER 22

EYES TO SEE

MAY 14, 1997

I cannot finish this book without relating the most wondrous, highly extraordinary experience of my life. It was at the dedication of our new church. During the ceremony there was a very strong presence of God as we were worshipping. All of a sudden I felt the skin on my face being pulled back. I had no control over it. No one was touching me. It reminded me of films I had seen in which astronauts were experiencing gravity force which caused such distortion to their face. I don't think it was to that extent, but it felt like it.

I wondered what on earth was happening. Some power, some force unknown to me caused the skin on my face to be pulled and moved in a way that I would not be able to do myself. I was bewildered.

Suddenly my spiritual eyes were opened and I saw Him! It was not a vision, it was real. I must have been transported to the spirit realm. Up on the platform in the front of the church on the left side there was a white-latticed archway entwined with beautiful flowers. To the side and back of Him were many beings that I perceived but could not see distinctly. I heard the words "the company of heaven."

Then Jesus walked through the portal and to the center of the stage. It took my breath away! He looked so majestic, regal, kingly, and royal. No king could ever have been dressed so magnificently. There He was, the Son of God, the King of kings, the Lord of lords, the Word become flesh, the Alpha and the Omega. In His hand He held the scepter of His divine authority. His face beamed and shone with the light of heaven. He smiled, receiving the worship and blessing the congregation according to NUMBERS 6:24–26: "The Lord bless thee and keep thee: The Lord make his face shine upon thee, and be gracious unto thee: The Lord lift up His countenance upon thee, and give thee peace."

His face was truly shining upon us! Then He seemed to turn into pure light. It was whiter than the whitest white I ever saw. It looked like a tangible substance. He is the light of the world.

After that I was back in the natural realm, weeping. The service had concluded and people were leaving but I could not move. Between sobs of ecstasy, I told my husband what I had seen. He wanted me to tell the pastor, so I did. The pastor said he was sure that the Lord had touched many of the people that day. My whole being trembled with joy and excitement. I left the church in awe and wonder and pondered this experience.